TOURING THE SHADOW FACTORY

TOURING THE SHADOW FACTORY

Gary Stein

Brick Road Poetry Press
www.brickroadpoetrypress.com

Cover art by rukawajung

Author photo: © Cathy Henderson

Library of Congress Control Number: 2019938976
ISBN: 978-0-9979559-8-9

Published by Brick Road Poetry Press
513 Broadway
Columbus, GA 31902-0751
www.brickroadpoetrypress.com

Brick Road logo by Dwight New

*Thanks to my wife, Cathy, the thoughtful first reader
of these poems whose encouragement has kept me writing,
and to my sons, Jesse and Eliot, who provided much raw material.
Also thanks to my poetry group, The New Room Poets.
Over many years their insights and suggestions
in our monthly sessions have improved my work.*

Table of Contents

I.

II.

I.

Living Near the Kill Van Kull

It began when your father's hand tiptoed
from your shoulder. What did you think in the dark?
Remember the whistle lifting off the locomotive
each night, that shrill call from the tracks.
Or the deep horn that warned the ferry from the hull,
plowing fog at the wet curve of earth.
How the warmth of the gone hand fades.

One night he forgot to flick the nightlight
when he went. That's the way it ends,
the way you learn to trust the solitude.
No lighthouse ever saved a blind sailor; no mother
ever saved a son from what she knows rail
and river bring, bring and take away.

Remembering the Rabbits

Every day at four the rabbits skittered crazy
in the pen for pellets while mother watched
her broken stove buckled in the corner
like a refugee. Every supper multiplied
confusion. Father used to shoot them in the head.

Memory is tricky, though I'm sure they hung
from rafters in the shed, shorn of skin, blue
meat and flies ready for the iron pan
above the oven door he sutured shut with wire.

I used to think it was the slaughtered meal
that stopped her fork. But now I dream Dad's bag
packed heavy on the porch, the sax slung
in its case, and, leaning on the house,
a rifle with notches on the butt and silent ricochet.

Have you ever heard a dying rabbit scream?
His alto sax could sound like that and make
your spine go tight. Mother didn't sing
all day, just pinned our laundry to the line.
White clothes, lonely for his jeans and ratty socks—
the space they would have hung from
filled up by the sky and what he didn't say.

Time Out

The night the clock fell off the wall
seconds ticked across the kitchen tile
like bits of glass and Momma ran them down.
We watched her elbows work the floor,
dress flapping as she broomed
the fractured hands into a bag.
The room came clean and Dad rammed shut
the door with his good arm and fled.
Then she cried and sent us off to sleep.
She took a week to hang another clock.
Remember how we heard electric time
hum and haunt the wall above the stove?
Then the dog we lost barked one night
beyond our sight. But we went back
to school like normal kids. And Dad
walked through the open door again,
his sax beneath his arm as if he'd never left.

Prey

The Oak Road boys pushed the bow into my hands
taunting me to take a life for them.
I aimed the arrow high above the squirrel
but low enough to let them think I wanted blood.

The squirrel stood still and hugged the trunk
steady as my pulse until I bent the bow
and snapped it loose. Then the squirrel leapt up
to meet a point in time and catch it in the back.

We watched it pinned to wood a while,
the way paws beat the bark as if to blame
the tree. Before the sky dropped down to fix
those eyes in cloud, it screamed.

It was the human pitch that scared the Oak Road
boys away, but I was stuck by sound until
it stopped. And when it stopped I stayed
more still and felt the rush of blood
veins arrowed at my heart to make me move.

Once, age four, I fell from bed at night
and lay there wild enough to yell the darkness
white, but no one came to put me back.
I hugged the floor in vain for what was lost
and beat my knuckles raw until at last
in that harder place I came alone to sleep.

What He Gave Up

I was six when the doctor froze his smoke.
So mother burned cartons of Luckies
like leaves in the alley ash can.
And dad's colors drained—
a brown from deep within his fingers,
the yellow etched into the marrow of his teeth.

I missed the crisp cellophane shards on the sofa
and the earthy autumn smell
rising from the cushions in his chair.
I missed the smoke seeped into his lungs,
how his chest filled at leisure
as the light dropped down the blinds
in the little room
slat by slat.

For months we wondered at his temper,
how he inhaled candy by the bag
until his face, reddened by loss
of that cloudy angel,
nearly burst into fire.

We forget sacrifices a father turns to habit,
a kind of faith:
hiding ashtrays, wiping walls of nicotine.

Thirty years later, when the cancer etched his bones,
he offered up his testicles,
buying time with living coin.
No doctor knew what magic part to cut out next,
and when he finally went

I'll bet it was his lungs that held
the final pink inside him.

Isn't it a measured paring down we do
to save a hazy corner of the future:
from our fattest appetite to the final
belt-hole in the leather—a cutting back
to smaller rooms, fewer steps, a slimmer
piece of fish, until there's little left
to choose between—us and just the air,
just the smoke we're bound for.

Touring The Shadow Factory

And here we keep the wall animals, ears for the most part
and sharp snouts children favor, formerly cast by hand.
Now we own the tools to put faces on dumb jaws
so mothers and fathers may flick a switch
and sneak from the room, fingers intact.

To the left are the darks of one million negatives.
We gauge the blackest parts to millimeters then,
by careful splicing, fit shadow to actual
buildings and let whole cities hide
from themselves, reduced to snapshots.

The CIA shows interest, but this room serves solely
to promote memory loss. Next are the white shadows
of the dying. Many a man wears one in rain or in his youth
to impress companions. The pope, it is said,
bought a pair to confound assassins,

the press of pious crowds, and pilgrims who claim
to have seen the Holy Ghost at his wake
in a puff of smoke. And finally we give you a souvenir,
the stuffing of dreams. Because of all the ways
you have shed skin, we will elaborate your death

for survivors. First, slip out of your clothes and forget
fifty years of sunlight; you melt without it.
When a puddle forms, we pump it through the lungs
of mushrooms and throw you black and grotesque
on the wall of someone who forgot you.

Something Useful

I.

One Saturday when I was fifteen,
Dad said I had to learn to make an ashtray.
So I trudged behind him down the cellar
where we nailed a small wood mold
for pounding that thin copper sheet into its shape
with the nob of a ballpeen hammer.

He got me started then watched me whack
the flat out of that metal till the pockmarks
married in the bowl. We didn't say much
beyond the borders of the job, just stood
together two hours under the dim tube light,
my arm pinging with the blows.

Then he cut strips and curved two copper
U's to rivet to the sides like fingers poised
to hold the pleasure he gave up just to save
his life. For the rest of your life, he said,
wherever you live you'll have something useful.

II.

Twenty years ago he died from a cancer
you can't catch from cigarettes. I've smoked
twice since then: once for fellowship and once
to see the glowing in the thing we made together.
I liked how the tip turned red with breathing
in the air, the way smoke curled and twisted
on itself like talk before it disappears, the way
it helps your time with friends across a table.

III.

Outside the crematorium I watched the air
until they gave us back the urn we buried
in a wall of World War vets, like those
he likely started smoking with in forty-four.

Now I own a home without a spark burn in the rug,
without a single ashtray on a single table.
Smokers have to stand outside to do it fast,
alone, and scatter ashes on the grass
or cup them in their palm.

Stick Shift

Because the girl could who taught you to Watusi
and your father could, too, who knotted

bowties into butterflies. Because your left leg
lay jealous of its strong twin and bored as a day

at the shore, sand-caked and still. The Beetle
faced uphill and you feared rolling back, blind

to the past. Then she said, feel, feel the friction point.
Press ahead, her hand on yours like a manual brain

until the right arm learns to think for itself.
This century forgets the feel of a fountain pen

flowing words, or a foamy shaving brush
on your face. Drive on, like a crusty used car

throttling into summer on Old Oak Lane,
a thruway now, back to that stiff clutch,

its stubborn failure to turn into something
like the lever that moves the world. You learn

to slip the clutch smooth as a heart that hits
high gear just in time to steer through the skid

in the miles that go both ways. Cruise beyond
the dead girl, the dead father and his long reach,

closer to whatever lies just around the bend.

One Night on the Porch at Meyer's Creek

The others, tired of picking meat
from blue-claw crabs, drifted inside,
leaving the pile to my dying father and me
as the sun and moon hung like an artist's mistake

on opposite sides of the same dusk.
We bent to our work with lips and nails—
sucking broken legs, digging mustard from carapace,
our fingers raw and slick as memory.

We didn't speak, but there was sound enough:
the crack of shell yielding to mallet; flicker
trapped in the lantern; moths beating the screen
for light; a lone outboard across the water

racing night home, and the slap-slap of its wake.
Darkness took all but the distance between us
across the plank table. When the lantern failed,
we ate by feel to the heartbeat of crickets

and warm beer whispering up the bottle's neck.
Finally we were ghosts in a gone place
with nothing, for once, to prove,
nothing to lose, sweetened by silence.

If sound weren't beyond us
there'd have come a humming in the dark.

Washing the Car

That last Thanksgiving the tumors
took a holiday. While the women
cleared turkey bones and salad plates,
he walked into warm November light.
Then he uncoiled a hose, sprayed
the Buick, sponged it and polished

circles in the chrome with the old
chamois from the trunk. And while
the coffee brewed, no one missed him
yet, though some of us caught this last
chore through the glass—one bent man
managing what work was left to do.

Perhaps he thought his place in time
depended on the order left behind,
turning metal into grace
that glinted in the moon
when a woman rolled her husband home
that night asleep in his clean car.

Building a Father

1.

My father's square hands waked the grace
in wood. After dinner he drifted downstairs
to lose himself in habit: to cobble a table,
pound true nails or turn legs on a lathe.

It's four years since we waded to your crypt
in rain, the boats of our shoes a memory
of the ships you drafted into life.
How we ferried you, ash dry, across the water.

2.

Something dwells in the teak grain
of this inlaid chess table, in the tongue-in-groove,
the beveled edge, or in that elegant octagonal
piece framed from a single board.
I never found the soul in wood. My pencil
only carves thin shadows in paper, translucent,
the eraser shavings piling like sawdust.

Every man needs a craft, you said,
but I shied from planks and joints and doubted
you wanted me bending your nails or dulling blades
downstairs where you labored precisely: a hook
for saws, pegs for chisels and awls, a rack
of bolts, each screw snug in its box, the sawdust swept
and kids tucked away. In the end you left me
baffling tools, solid furniture, orderly love.

3.

Father, you still escape, though I follow you down
to the silent workshop—faithfully hammering
words in straight lines, measured,
dove-tailed. My sons waiting in the hall
may find my poems one day and bend,
like me, to shape a father from his work, haunted
by the door the words were born behind or
wondering why he built so many worlds to hide in.

After We Replaced the Bay Window

It gets dark early in winter
when I drive up toward the warm
yellow light from the kitchen.

I see more clearly now
through the new glass
a woman facing out, her back

to the stove, reading at the white
table where a stubby candle burns.
She can't see me walking

up the long blacktop
perhaps watched by a deer
from the pine shadows.

She can't see me walking
from the darkest part
of the year toward my seat

on the other side of the candle
she lit at 6:00 to read or maybe
to see me differently.

The Cremationist's Day Off

After hours my neighbor turns out
the lights and slips from the crematorium
locking up fresh dead for the night.

When rowing those pilgrims across
the river of flame, he wears a lab coat
and asbestos gloves, wields a long
metal oar to paddle waves of memory.

And after the blazing white torrent,
sometimes skeletal nobs remain—
shoulders and hips—until the giant
compactor grinds bone to dust.
He says survivors fear finding
the familiar in the part of death
celebrated on the mantel.

While the ovens rest, the neighbor
squats in his garden, the wildest on the block,
wearing plaid shorts and black socks,
an ordinary guy teasing tender green
shoots from knuckle-deep loam.

When he thinks no one is looking,
he lifts his hand to sniff
the darkness under his nails.

In the Country, Deer

Each night deer wander from the woods,
fan out, each to a different house,
a different window, waiting
for a woman to wake to their stare.

Once, from her bedroom, Anne saw eyes
in the dark, through bubbled glass,
a prism of rain. Some say God
watches every move. Through the window

of heaven, He sees our thoughts as if
the skull were His theater. He knows
the hour of the last breath of every last
soul until the end of time.

In the country is no theater, no zoo.
The walls of a cottage appear.
The deer watch Anne kneel by her bed.
Nostrils flare, ears twitch.

The deer wait for her to pray,
sing in her cage, or flick a switch
to cover herself in a blanket of light.
Each night the next miracle.

Hansel Remembers Famine

after Louise Glück

Gretel said shadows are souls
that whisper like leaves blowing.
Hungry mothers must eat
what they hate, what they love most.

Of course we ran. Night has no arms
to comfort the young. Even the dark
ached for its meal. Footsteps in the
forest. Ours? Crows stole the crumbs.

Maybe children need to be lost
to find their way. Was the house
made of cake? Did mice eat
the eaves? Yes the blind old lady

baked and the brick oven bled
red heat. Gretel said she burned
a witch. Memory can lie
but I remember a chicken bone,

the rich smell of bread, a heaven
of smoke but no screams.
Mother, may God rest her soul,
never knew what happened.

Geppetto Remembers

The soul that entered pine entered
on my blade. The hand that held
the chisel honed each toe, bent
the knee, rubbed the stain

that turned to skin. I had to nail
your hands to string and hang you
from a board to train your limbs.
How slow the dancer learns his steps.

My father worked in wood and what
he never nailed me to
works my tongue as well as string.
What a puppet says is second hand.

I wanted you to look like me
but force me to improve; to speak a word
I've never heard; stay safe
at home; be brave enough to leave.

Pino, whales are real. Fathers
can be whales that swallow us
like krill, then sound beneath the waves.
A lucky man has a son

to gather sticks, tunnel down a throat
and light a flame
to make the monster sneeze
hard enough to save them both.

Winding Father's Watch

Through the crystal bezel twelve thin lines
deny the hours their numbers. Slim, gold,
Swiss-made miracle on my wrist.
Each morning twist the stem to start

the future. A needle pries open the back case:
pinion, pallet, gears with teeth, spring
and jewel, the spinning wheels men made
to tell us when to eat, when to close our eyes.

Time is tricky when you're eight: the past
still ticks. Little fingers spun hands backward:
bring back Christmas, the lost dog,
the forgotten life before leaving God for earth.

Father said the mechanism mimics the heavens
rolling forward forever. *We name what happens
"time"*—a noun we cannot touch, but I can hold
his gift: two steady hands from long ago in mine.

Darkroom

You float up beneath my fingers.
I rub old sun into your hair,
hear bees bother our meal beyond the lens.
In the dust-free air it is grass again;
it is years ago, not this small night.
Your image whispers itself in silver,
the echo so perfect I leave the room.

Cleaning the Wood Out Under the Porch

for Mark

My friend listens to wood say, *Free me*
from too many shapes. He crooks each board
to the shoulder and rifles his eye down,
ear cocked. He says, *This edge is true,*
the grain tight, an old plank, probably oak.
Keep this. Someday you'll be glad.

I say, *Take it.* I don't know how
to turn anything into anything. To me
it's a home for bent nails. Just wood
with hard rain coming.

Most of it is junk already: the roof
of a dog's house, the end of cabinets.
We shove it back under to burn
next winter and shove back a few good
boards my friend respects too much to take.

Carpentry must have come easy
to Jesus with his many fathers
and mysterious ways. The rest of us work
for slow miracles: grapes that bloom
in the cask; one fish at a time;
the fetus beneath the sea.

How easily my friend's faith shapes
me: the good wood rooting beneath
the porch splinter by splinter.

Sailing with My Father

On a perfect day they say you glide
to Orchard Shoals without a fight.
And when that good air fills the cloth
you jam your sheets. The sky will lift you up.

Forty years ago you ranged this very bay.
The boat was your design, and you
conjured up a son to man the jib that pulls
across an ocean's pulse.

Today our rigid backs are leaping fish
hiked out and fixed against the sea,
against the speckled light.

A humming fills my head. The boat heels
its quivered oak so far from shore
we disappear upwind. You want the earth
to end in spray. You want this day,
its ancient foam across the bow,
to hand the tiller down.

I say jibe her over. I am not your dream
and taste the salt along raw lips.
This boat however true it's hulled
isn't my invention. Shove the tiller hard
aweather. It's time to reach for home.

His Last October

That was the night when the body forgot
its disguise, the old costume fled the attic
and father lay in his electric bed.

An old tree sheds twigs like hair,
like memory. Children in wild wigs
run loose, chasing mystery and sugar

palms out, while one man
finally untethered, turns blue
from the toes up. After the clock chokes

on its own number, who lets the air in?
When night seeps through the eyes
the tongue forgets its dance.

As the blue licked at his knees
we struggled like blind worms flushed
by rain, stranded in light. Don't children stop

at the edge of the woods? Don't saints
hold out their hands? Then the nurse said:
What's farthest from the heart dies first.

Identifying the Body

At the morgue, dead are reduced
to a face, horizontal,
smaller than life.

My father: grey-orange
handsome, not cold.
I touched the hard cheek
and remember him
even in my fingers.

Love, you could not view
your mother.

After twenty-five years
I remember her both ways, still.
Loss is persistent as bone.

When they raise the sheet on me
do this last kind thing:
tell them, *That's him,*
my husband.

Husband once meant *tiller*
of soil or master of the house
but words have more lives
than skin.

Just say, *Yes.*
I will be in your hands.

Hindsight

If you look over your shoulder
to see what's behind you
a neck swivels only
so far into the past.

If you turn your head
the finch pecking thistle
at the feeder out the window
turns to memory

and the dark puddles
from yesterday's rain
are air today the way
ghosts evaporate.

While in the cemetery
of the dead and their dead
the beautiful earth
brims thick with bones.

II.

This Afterlife

Children play dead so well
because the past calls them.
Their tiny heads burrow
lightly into the warm sand
at the shore of words.
Remember how you hid

under blankets, how you closed
the eyes of the world?
How you crouched in the closet
thick with wet wool
and camphor at the edge
of the murmuring room?

Ghosts spy on parents
from every corner of the house,
on the bodies they are sent
to fill as they wait
for waves of light
to push them through the door.

The Rabbit's Tumor

George turned nine on Easter, lump-chested.
The vet sliced off one hard grape and left
little sprouting nobs too numerous for knives.
He laid odds at ninety-five percent and hawked
a forty-dollar test to type the tumor.
We chose ignorance, chose to leave
George's doom unnamed and the children
five percent of hope. Only humans have to know
death's date of birth, the bullet's very number.
Rodents simply drop. So our old pet rests
his stitches in the pen, nibbling pears
while the boys watch what a rabbit does until it dies.
My father ended just as sweet, favoring
Italian ice to meat, his tumor staged down
to the hour hunger stopped. Then we watched
his glucose drip. One day my sons must turn
from my bed too, blink and wonder how to weigh
each ragged breath. They'll take what they want
of father falling off the bone of memory,
summon grace they practiced by the hutch,
then, famished, flee downstairs to lunch.

Dysentery

When the third child in three months
died by dehydration
the mother saw signs
and summoned my camera to her dirt hut
where a chicken strutted guard
near the little corpse.

She laid him out for Easter
in blue satin, his straw hat
in his cold fist, candles and tortillas
wrapped in last year's news
to light and fortify his soul.

Padre said the Nahuatl
were ignorant of hygiene.
*Don't feed superstition
with snapshots of the dead.*

But photos were all I had to offer grief
and when the flash lit the dark walls
the mother laughed.
*Make the white light come again.
Make it come back.*

The print came back
weeks later from a New York lab.
I sent it down believing
she would see her son again
but not his faint halo of flies.

All Hallows' Eve

for Helen

I've made a habit of dead men's coats
but had to cut my father's down

to size and wore it till the thread went thin.
It died two years after him.

The tailor could not fit me
to my father, the better handyman

and reader of the wind and tide.
His clothes just kept me warm.

But I have hope for David's cloth.
I thought he was shorter in the sleeves

but this tweed fits me like my own
and has a soft hand like his

on piano keys. I'll hear more Bach,
choose wine with greater care,

and better watch the small things
in the world. Tonight as children

chase, palms out, the souls I've lost
run loose until I try them on again.

Watching the Goalie

Is it better that you don't hear my small voice
in the din of parents stalking the sideline?
I doubt you need more frantic instructions.
Why, at eleven, would you want a job
that permits no fear or hesitation—
each Saturday a chance for glory
or utter desolation. What drove you
to be "the man" who must save ten
when they fail? You dive flat against the air,
skidding your face on dirt, slide-tackle
bigger boys until last week's scabs tear loose
and run red. When you fly from the net
in a chaos of dust and thunder feet,
I almost look away. I can understand
the elation of a sliding save, the punch-out
three feet higher than your head,
the penalty kick ripped down before
we guess which way to jump,
when every mother's scream bears your name.
But the cold loneliness of the last man
when one scuts by your straining arms.
How can you rise from your knees
to face the next volley of feet?
Perhaps I fear you will learn fear
and, fearing, lose the blind instinct
that saves everything. What can save
the goalie if he doubts the magic
synapse that prods another dad
to ask, "Who is that? That kid in goal?"
I want to tell him but stay quiet—I don't

know who lives in your skin or how you grew
that heart. Is there a word for joy
that moves along the spine? Listen: my mute
chest shouts your name like a crowd, hoping
that wild faith might live on even in me.

Jesse's Song

The quiet boy, sixteen, who toddled young but never crawled,
once subluxed his knee pitching a ball, the patella slicing foul,
fractured a finger in the car door, a toe against a stove, walked
a nail through his foot, tore two ligaments stepping off a curb,

was borne twice in agony from a soccer field, once an ice rink,
once the school hall, sweated crutches three straight summers
and saw eyes drilled through a pumpkin knee, now breaks
the news he's cast in the school musical to sing tenor,

tap dance and tango, hurl girls high, catch them and tumble
across the stage. We've only seen his quads spasm, not dance.
We've only heard his young voice scale the strained register
of pain. So we clutch our tickets, shouldering in like

Lourdes' pilgrims, counting braces and bloody bandages
abandoned at the footlights, hoping to see one body translate
itself into an ordinary star. If it's our sure applause he wills
his new self for, this act's enough for me to upstage fear,

grow my lost hair back, mock death or, at least,
drag from bed once more and dance my weary ass to work.

One Hour After Curfew

Kitchen tiles numb my feet to the ankle bone.
Six times a minute the faucet drips and somewhere in the joists
that old mouse scrabbles for a way into our grain.

Somewhere on the rain-slick parkway, our teen careens,
wipers broken bird legs, but it's me immobilized.

Once he floated where we tucked him in the crib—
angelfish in a tank waiting for our eyes to swim
through the glass—that close to an understanding.

Now they say distance is the point, the letting go success.
The car shrinking so far down the road you can't make out

the model. I stumble the cluttered garage like a drunk
to find the metal box and throw the circuit breakers
one by one and feel the house shudder down—floor by floor

beneath my palm. Good night rumbled furnace; good night
pilot light, humming stove, and luminescent face of time
    unplugged.

Listen. When he bumbles with the door lock, it's me
gone taut in the wing-back chair. When every switch he flicks
fails, it's me. In the foyer in the gloom of missing

rhythm, cold currents worm across the floor.
Let this silent house gather in his ears a sound like all my fears

for him. Let him hear my even breathing closing in.
In that frozen moment he won't know just where I am,
what's gone wrong, or what will happen next.

Labor Day

The youngest flew to college last week.
Time to re-order my own life.

I begin with the penny box.
Twenty years of commerce leave

a pile of copper—worthless
but the kids used to run

their fingers through the coins,
learning how to treasure.

It takes time to push the coins down
flat in those brown wrappers

or they'll stand on edge and skew
the whole cylinder. Your finger

goes green and you wonder
if in the dazed monotony

a rare specimen sneaks through,
a valuable piece

bound for a distant bank vault.
You could invest years scanning

tiny price lists while pennies
overflow the drawer, so you take

your profit from the feel of a task
completed. The rolls mound up,

the pile rising like the inches
we etched each year on the door

our sons grew against, passed through.

Tree House

Built to free the boys from bed and board,
their careful parents. We let the stars
be our eyes, soft air tuck them in.

The bundle of bolts, joints and nails
that held them steady in the breeze
freed us for nights of our other selves.

Now outgrown as their bruised soccer cleats
it stands like a vagrant in our yard
hoping for a handout or a coat of varnish.

So I climb the ladder to their old fort,
their spaceship, their tower, and duck
my head to enter a window of air.

I place my pallet on the splintered slats
sagging with a man's weight, trusting
what we built on faith in the branches.

Long has this castle waited for me
to take possession, to dream in my sons' place:
the imaginary kingdom of time.

The Three-Fingered Cashier

At seventeen she could have been a stock-clerk
knifing cardboard in the Drug-Rite back room,
shelving ointment and orthopedic girdles
after hours, before the first fist of dawn opens
the door, opens her secret as if her sex,
to the whole sniggery world.

But they put her out front, back to the window
where the sun strikes her hand with every
punch of the register, every flapping open a paper
sack to the pills and salves we think we need.

It is because of her flowering smile that our eyes,
too, bloom way above that gnarled root,
that twisted smirk of a hand, for which she must
have died and died again every day of junior high.
And for the rest of her life she can smile
for nothing, bless our coins with those
three busy fingers, and offer us a kind of cure.

Adam Forgives Eve

The world was newer than names.
Even the trees opened their arms.

And Eve opened, and the serpent's tongue split
the apple flesh from skin and black seeds

at the heart. She said we could come
to understand sky, the way an eye opens

on morning, the way I went blind
with pleasure. She said we would see

in the dark. She wanted to make me better.
How can I blame her when she loved me

more than a God I can't understand?
Would I have done different?

She said we two can fill the earth
with nothing but feeling

and ripe fruit. This deep shudder
is worth a world of loss.

Adam Remembers the Serpent

I should have flattered Eve more, learned to dance
to fight the boredom, should have mocked
the glib line she took like a hungry fish.

Now we know forked tongues don't talk.
Was he just her dream? One of God's windstorm
tricks? The snake looked like a stick to me.

It moved so many ways at once just like
her hips. She hummed to him while I hid
behind a tree and wondered where we were,

whom to trust. A God we could not see
had ribbed her from me, a mystic surgeon's gift,
but His words slithered off her back like rain.

Lost in shame: for years we scratched for grain
with rats, and babies tore her guts. We screamed
octaves at each other and called it song.

Then one day she said there must be more
to earth than Eden and showed me how a flower
blooms from dirt. And when the children laugh

or we taste the leavened loaf, we cobble back
a fragment of a perfect world while living humbly
here where wind is only wind, a stick is just a stick.

At the Mercy of Flowers

for Dr. Woodrow C. Henderson

The coroner wrote, *cardiac arrest*,
death's signature disguise,
secondary to bee sting.

My wife made rare by God's ironic twist:
water carried life along our river house
but venom tricked her lungs to flood her out.

So many springs she knelt down
on a rubber pad in dirt
to mulch and prune, plant and graft,

an innocent woman, loving
hard at the mercy of flowers
that colored our table: a gift of bees.

We beat the risks we knew:
being poor in towns too small
for news; the bombs of World War II;

raising kids without a net;
trusting the vanquished air.
We never feared that she would live

too short or me so long
that I've outlived my work,
our friends, two years of rage,

the four I wrestled with regret.
Now I hire eyes to read to me
how we won the war,

show me photos of myself in France
through a magnifying glass.
I've come to think that time

has turned me blind to all
that isn't past, and I totter through
the yard as if on stilts in fog—

drunk on time. But after all
I still spoon honey in my tea,
smell bouquets without a pause

and think of her and God
among the blooms, and even
in the buzzing that they hide.

Travels in Time

In memory of Elizabeth Henderson 1913–1980

That day you found a shoot off the ajuga
demanding scissors: a small thread in air
that only insects and one who loved nature
and order could see. As you snipped, a bee
neatly found the fine line running
through your finger into the future.

If each of us has a double in nature,
yours might have been the bee: your
pantry heavy with honey, the gardens
that seemed to follow your steps
so closely you shared a blur of color.
You too made much with little visits.

That is how it was when the bee
telegraphed its message through your blood.
I see you wading in flowers, waving off
the bees as always on a hot day at the river
although you knew there was no medicine
for the right sting. That is how it must be

for all of us who dwell with forces
that but for one moment serve us.
At the grave in shimmering heat, a fetus
beats against the dark as your daughter
knits with needles of blood new bone: a pilgrim
from spent centuries to the long unknown.

Smoke Rings

Nonno preferred *Antonio e Cleopatra*
and each morning packed four Corona
in the breast pocket of his tweed jacket,
a plucked flower peeking from the lapel,
on his way downtown to the workbench
where he fashioned gems and metal
into art women wanted to wear.

Once at home he poured a tiny bag
of raw diamonds into my small palm.
He said each bore its own color and shape
just like people, each stone ancient
formed by magic in the ground.
At eight I knew the early earth sparkled.

Then in his wicker chair he lit up
and poked my finger through the rings
before they spiraled toward heaven,
home then for Nonna, dead one year,
waiting for us or at least our prayers.

Now, sixty years gone, near my garden chair
wren and finch still flit and blooms
ready to pluck wave in soft air. Smoke
rising from my Robusto catches in the light
of this poem. Like the gold band from his hands
on my finger, still there, still here.

Grooming

Some believe this blizzard to be God's judgment,
thirty-six hours of white wind erasing earth
and night, punishing our darkness.

My steel shovel bites and bites, shaving
inches off the drifts while my beard goes untamed:
one important chore abandoned for another.

I remember Grandfather at the bathroom mirror,
bowl and brush in hand. He'd free his straight blade
from its sheath to strop against the leather strip

chained to the sink. Then came the scraping.
Years later I'd squirt canned foam and grip
the Gillette Father felt could cause less harm

in careful hands. Short strokes work best, he said,
pull tight your cheek, shave against the grain. Now
I rub this stubbled chin and watch sky fill up the earth.

Just a Trim

The Vietnamese woman
who snips my hair
in Andre's Salon
was just a child when
our planes flamed
her village.

Now she calls herself
"Ann," the ghost
of a name. Eight
thousand miles from
home her busy blades
whirl over

my small head.
For twenty bucks
she tries to tame
the thin forest
of time's gentle
defoliation.

Jogging

You drag by the knees before
learning the secret of toes, and running
comes last in the slow lessons
the leg unwinds. In time pain
stops and the body becomes your own
idea; breath becomes sky and the soul
floats out from all dull pumping.

At a great distance you hear feet
ticking, just as the earth must. You
think nothing can stop this machinery
but even little deaths end. The soul
climbs down to its tree and legs
thicken into summer.

In this white season you stick
to the sheets and want to leave
your body again. You practice breathing,
set your shoes ready and twist
the clocksprings tight by the pillow.
Every hour the curtain flutters
but you remain inside
drowning in knots, jealous of fish.

We want a summer to explode, good
death, space that is still. Why when
you run out of a body for miles
is there any more?

The Undertow: Hatteras Island

And as many times as the ocean curls
itself into an arm and slams
me to shore scattering
memory like dice, I bob up, smiling
postcards and snake my body sideways
to the breakers for another throw.

Reason should prevail or the pain
of knees scraping the shore of all
its shells. But I am leaning out, letting
the undertow suck me down the beach,
laughing like pebbles in the foam.

You may say this idiot's dance,
this giddy, numb surrender to the moon
is what we face each morning—
snake eyes teasing with another chance.

It is not. We predict the ocean now.
If you gauge the tides, the wind, and chart
the bottom you can call a wave down
to the inch. But knowing doesn't ease
the ride, doesn't tell you how you'll
hit the sand or when to close your eyes.

Forget the ways we know. The undertow
is a kind of yearning. Perhaps this poem
is a shell. It is a shell. Gather it
around your ear until you hear surf, faintly,

as far as the moon, but surf. Surf.
Each distant wave carries
further from the beach.

Bifocals

Age alters our vision,
says the headlamped ophthalmologist
blinding into my retina.
It happens at the age you are.

The focal machinery loses elasticity.
Arms compensate like the bellows of antique
cameras, sliding objects up and back
until fuzz recedes magically
turning peaches to plums. *Voila!*
There are so many ways to digest light.

The physics of optical distortion
corrects reality or restores it—
depending on point of view.
They grind lenses precisely now
without the telltale line. They hide
one frail organ after another,
until one white day you die all at once
from the weight of your disguises.

Remember this: for reading and fine
work look down close to your heart.
For the long view, for the signs from
a distant highway, look up and away.

Sometimes, during my period of adjustment
I confuse distance with the faint beating
beneath my eyes and hesitate at the margins
of the lenses, at the subtle crystal curve,
at the soft blur of my future.

Subway

When cities swell
with business, cramping
motion, men flow

through stone, pulsed
blood beneath skin.
The river parts

and we rattle the *Times*
in our fast seats, invisible
as a stranger's dream,

nodding on the aisle.
We lean toward each
stop as if with hope

while the train transfuses
itself. What enters
the heart enters between

beats. Above us doors
and faces wait to open
to our rising like flowers

dreaming. Sun blooms
over each stem at the same
deliberate speed. We

travel the winking lights
of the tunnel,
space between darkness.

On the Rodanthe Fishing Pier

A puff took my lucky hat
with the feather poked
in the grommet

over the spindly wooden rail.
My son, scared, looked
from my pale head

to that ragged hat gulling away
under the bald August sun.
Another gust

ballooned it higher
before it floated down,
hit the crest of a whitecap,

and rode the swell,
a cotton jockey for seconds
then ducked at the finish

under a green wave.
It was my father's hat,
gone before I could raise

my arms. The fish my son caught
he threw back to the ocean.

Cleaning the Catch

I.

When the twitching ends,
or better before, scrape
with the flat of your blade,
let the gritty scales fly and root
in the hair of your arm. Slit
behind the pectoral, sever the head.

Gash a thin line from belly
to anus, spill the guts:
look for eggs, so good
in butter and lemon.
Irrigate the cavity.

II.

Though you scrub with vinegar
and soap, you may wake
to scales in your bed
and beneath your nails
the rank odor of fish.
On your breath its breath.

What's stolen from a river haunts.
Again the arcing rainbow,
a lure locked on its lips, its agony
and death-smell return.
No fish is as simple as its body.
Once we too lived inches from air.

On My 50th Birthday

The path ribbons six miles
through a gift of woods. I run
slow as a leaf turning red
to read seasons and the mood
of the creek between rain.
Are signs given or must we scour
earth for shreds of light?

At the old bend a doe peeks
from a stand of pine ten yards
from my ticking feet, its tense nose
reading me in a language I'll never know.
Sometimes, lost in myself like her,
I'm startled by speed, by the rattle
of traffic crossing the far bridge
or the hawk's shadow circling
my ragged breath in the wind.

Five miles done, redundant as a mantra,
close to home, I run toward
moments of grace, the surprise
of old friends crouching in the dark
of my house, candles waiting to bloom.

Acknowledgments

The following poems first appeared elsewhere, some in slightly different form:

Antietam Review: "One Hour After Curfew," & "Watching the Goalie"

Asheville Poetry Review: "Geppetto Remembers"

Baltimore Review: "Building a Father"

Folio: "Bifocals"

Gargoyle: "The Cremationist's Day Off"

Journal of the American Medical Association: "Prey," "At The Mercy of Flowers," "Travels in Time," "Dysentery," "Identifying the Body," "One Night On The Porch at Meyer's Creek," "The Rabbit's Tumor," "The Three-Fingered Cashier," "This Afterlife," "Washing the Car," "What He Gave Up," "His Last October," & "Jesse's Song"

Little Patuxent Review: "Tree House"

Poet Lore: "Living Near The Kill Van Kull," "Remembering the Rabbits," "Just A Trim," "Hindsight"

Poetry: "Subway"

Potomac Review: "Sailing With My Father"

Prairie Schooner: "Darkroom"

The Poet Upstairs: "The Undertow: Hatteras Island"

The Sow's Ear: "All Hallows' Eve" & "Stick Shift"

The Washington Review: "Cleaning the Wood Out Under the Porch"

A few of these poems also appeared in the chapbook, *Between Worlds*, which was a finalist in the Finishing Line Press annual open chapbook competition (2014).

About the Author

Gary Stein's poems have appeared or are forthcoming in *Poetry*, *Prairie Schooner*, *Poet Lore*, *Folio*, *The Sow's Ear*, *The Asheville Poetry Review*, *Atlanta Review*, *Gargoyle*, and numerous other journals and anthologies. His chapbook, *Between Worlds* (Finishing Line Press, 2014), was a finalist in the publisher's annual national competition. Gary's work has also been nominated for a Pushcart Prize. He holds an M.F.A. from the Iowa Writer's Workshop, served three years as Book Review Editor of *Poet Lore*, and co-edited the poetry anthology: *Cabin Fever* (The Word Works, 2004). Gary has taught Creative Writing in colleges and high schools, and he currently practices law in the D.C. metropolitan area where he and his wife have raised two sons.

Our Mission

BRICK ROAD

POETRY PRESS

The mission of Brick Road Poetry Press is to publish and promote poetry that entertains, amuses, edifies, and surprises a wide audience of appreciative readers. We are not qualified to judge who deserves to be published, so we concentrate on publishing what we enjoy. Our preference is for poetry geared toward dramatizing the human experience in language rich with sensory image and metaphor, recognizing that poetry can be, at one and the same time, both familiar as the perspiration of daily labor and as outrageous as a carnival sideshow.

Available from Brick Road Poetry Press

www.brickroadpoetrypress.com

Treading Water with God by Veronica Badowski

Rich Man's Son by Ron Self

Just Drive by Robert Cooperman

The Alp at the End of My Street by Gary Leising

The Word in Edgewise by Sean M. Conrey

Household Inventory by Connie Jordan Green

Practice by Richard M. Berlin

A Meal Like That by Albert Garcia

Cracker Sonnets by Amy Wright

Things Seen by Joseph Stanton

Battle Sleep by Shannon Tate Jonas

Lauren Bacall Shares a Limousine by Susan J. Erickson

Ambushing Water by Danielle Hanson

Having and Keeping by David Watts

Assisted Living by Erin Murphy

Credo by Steve McDonald

The Deer's Bandanna by David Oates

Also Available from Brick Road Poetry Press

www.brickroadpoetrypress.com

Dancing on the Rim by Clela Reed

Possible Crocodiles by Barry Marks

Pain Diary by Joseph D. Reich

Otherness by M. Ayodele Heath

Drunken Robins by David Oates

Damnatio Memoriae by Michael Meyerhofer

Lotus Buffet by Rupert Fike

The Melancholy MBA by Richard Donnelly

Two-Star General by Grey Held

Chosen by Toni Thomas

Etch and Blur by Jamie Thomas

Water-Rites by Ann E. Michael

Bad Behavior by Michael Steffen

Tracing the Lines by Susanna Lang

Rising to the Rim by Carol Tyx

About the Prize

The Brick Road Poetry Prize, established in 2010, is awarded annually for the best book-length poetry manuscript. Entries are accepted August 1st through November 1st. The winner receives $1000 and publication. For details on our preferences and the complete submission guidelines, please visit our website at www.brickroadpoetrypress.com.

Winners of the Brick Road Poetry Prize

2017
Touring the Shadow Factory by Gary Stein

2016
Assisted Living by Erin Murphy

2015
Lauren Bacall Shares a Limousine by Susan J. Erickson

2014
Battle Sleep by Shannon Tate Jonas

2013
Household Inventory by Connie Jordan Green

2012
The Alp at the End of My Street by Gary Leising

2011
Bad Behavior by Michael Steffen

2010
Damnatio Memoriae by Michael Meyerhofer

CPSIA information can be obtained
at www.ICGtesting.com
Printed in the USA
FSHW020011210619
59240FS

9 780997 955989